FIRST SPORTS SOURCE

FIRST SOURCE TO

BASKETBALL

RULES, EQUIPMENT, AND KEY PLAYING TIPS

by Tyler Omoth

First Facts®

CAPSTONE PRESS
a capstone imprint

First Facts are published by Capstone Press,
1710 Roe Crest Drive, North Mankato, Minnesota 56003
www.mycapstone.com

Library of Congress Cataloging-in-Publication Data
Cataloging-in-publication information is on file with the Library of Congress
ISBN 978-1-4914-8422-7 (library binding)
ISBN 978-1-4914-8431-9 (paperback)
ISBN 978-1-4914-8426-5 (eBook PDF)

Editorial Credits
Mandy Robbins, editor; Heidi Thompson, designer; Eric Gohl, media researcher;
Lori Blackwell, production specialist

Photo Credits
Dreamstime: Eric Broder Van Dyke, 9, Paskee, cover; Getty Images: Anadolu Agency, 11, Doug Pensinger, 19, NBAE/Steve Freeman, 17; Newscom: Cal Sport Media/Albert Pena, 1, EPA/Michael Reynolds, 13 (right), Icon SMI, 21, MCT/David Santiago, 5, USA Today Sports/Dan Hamilton, 15, USA Today Sports/David Richard, 7, ZUMA Press/Kyndell Harkness, 13 (left); Shutterstock: Aspen Photo, 20, Torsak Thammachote, 1 (background)

Design Elements: Shutterstock

Printed and bound in the United States.
009368CGS16

TABLE OF CONTENTS

INTRODUCTION
Get in the Game!

Imagine being able to shoot like National Basketball Association (NBA) star Stephen Curry. What are you waiting for? Grab a ball and hit the court! Basketball is an exciting, fast-paced sport to play. This game doesn't require much equipment—just a lot of energy!

FACT
The first rulebook for basketball contained only 13 rules. The 2014–2015 NBA rulebook has 66 pages of detailed rules.

INTERESTING ORIGINS

Dr. James Naismith invented basketball in 1891. The physical education teacher was looking for a way to keep students active between football and baseball seasons. The game was originally played with a soccer ball and peach baskets.

STEPHEN CURRY

CHAPTER 1
Ready to Play!

Equipment

To play basketball, all you need is a basketball, sneakers, and a basketball hoop. A regulation NBA basketball is 29.5 inches (75 centimeters) around. You can start out with a smaller ball until you get the hang of **dribbling** and shooting. Be sure to wear supportive athletic shoes. Good shoes protect your ankles.

FACT
Converse All-Stars were the first shoes made just for basketball. The first pair was made in 1917.

dribble—to bounce the ball with one hand

The Basketball Court

A basketball court is rectangular with a basketball hoop on each end. An NBA court is 94 feet (29 meters) long by 50 feet (15 m) wide. Lines mark the **free throw** line, three-point line, and half-court line. Many courts have wood flooring, but some are made of rubber material. Outdoor courts are made of concrete or **asphalt**.

free throw—a free shot taken from the free-throw line after a foul

asphalt—a black tar that is mixed with sand and gravel to make paved roads

FACT

The three-point shot was adopted by the NBA during the 1979—1980 season. To score a three-pointer, a player must shoot from behind the three-point arc. This line is 23 feet, 9 inches (7.2 m) away from the hoop.

CHAPTER 2
How the Game Works

A basketball team has five players on the court at a time. Each team has a hoop on one end of the court. To score points players put the ball into the basket for their team. Each player has a position. These include a point guard, a shooting guard, two forwards, and a center. The point guard focuses on ball handling and passing. The tallest teammate is usually the center.

"Basketball is a simple game ... get the ball close to the basket, and there are three ways to do that. Pass, dribble, and offensive rebound."

–*Phil Jackson,*
Hall of Fame coach

Playing Offense

Players move the ball by dribbling, passing, or shooting. To dribble they bounce the ball while walking or running. There are several types of passes. These include the overhead pass, chest pass, and bounce pass. **Jump shots** and **layups** are common ways to score. If a shot bounces off the backboard into the hoop, it's called a bank shot.

FACT
Kareem Abdul-Jabbar scored a record 38,387 career points in the NBA. Tina Thompson holds the Women's National Basketball Association (WNBA) record with 7,488 points.

jump shot—a basketball shot taken mid-jump
layup—a close shot where the ball is gently played off the backboard and into the hoop

JUMP SHOT

LAYUP

Defense

While on defense, one team tries to keep the other from scoring. Blocking an opponent's shot is a good way to stop him. Sometimes players swat the ball away or catch an opponent's pass. But defenders can't touch the person with the ball or they'll get called for a **foul**.

FACT
After receiving five fouls in one game, a player is removed from the game. This is called fouling out.

foul—to do an action in basketball that is against the rules; pushing and tripping are fouls

CHAPTER 3
Rules of the Game

Scoring

Players pass the ball a lot to keep the defense moving. This helps create openings for players to take shots at the basket. A standard basket is worth two points. If a player is fouled, he or she can take a free throw shot for one point. Shots made from beyond the three-point line are worth three points.

"To win the big games you must get to the free throw line, and then you must make them"

–Rick Majerus,
Hall of Fame coach

Regulation Time

A basketball game is made up of four quarters or two halves. In the NBA quarters are 12 minutes long. After two quarters the teams take a break at halftime. Games that are tied at the end of regulation time go into overtime. In the NBA overtime is five minutes.

FACT
A shot clock limits each team's possession time. The NBA has a 24-second shot clock.

12:08
24
EDDIE'S KIDS
NEW ORLEANS
23
HOLIDAY
11
42
59
SPALDING
AVAYA
AVAYA
AVAYA

Playing Tips

Now that you know the basics of basketball you can start building your skills. These tips can help.

PASSING

Using the bounce pass is a good way to get the ball to a teammate. By bouncing the ball off the court with a quick pass, you can avoid the defender's hands. If your teammate is running, make sure to pass the ball where he or she will be instead of where he or she currently is. This is called leading your receiver.

SHOOTING

Try to use one hand to shoot and the other to guide the ball. With a good follow-through your shooting hand should finish straight ahead of you. The ball should have **backspin** as it soars toward the hoop.

FACT

The Naismith Memorial Basketball Hall of Fame honors the greatest people in basketball history. The museum is located in Springfield, Massachusetts.

backspin—a backward rotation of the ball

Glossary

asphalt (AS-fawlt)—a black tar that is mixed with sand and gravel to make paved roads

backspin (BACK-spin)—a backward rotation of the ball

dribble (DRI-buhl)—to bounce the ball with one hand

foul (FOWL)—to do an action in basketball that is against the rules; pushing and tripping are fouls

free throw (FREE THROH)—a free shot taken from the free-throw line after a foul

jump shot (JUMP SHOT)—a basketball shot taken mid-jump

layup (LAY-up)—a close shot where the ball is gently played off the backboard and into the hoop

shoot (SHOOT)—to throw the ball toward the hoop in an attempt to score

Read More

Doeden, Matt. *All About Basketball*. All About Sports. North Mankato, Minn.: Capstone Press, Capstone Press, 2015.

Rivkin, Jennifer. *All Ball: Basketball's Greatest Players*. Basketball Source. New York: Crabtree Publishing Company, 2016.

Storden, Thom. *Amazing Basketball Records*. Epic Sports. North Mankato, Minn.: Capstone Press, 2015

Internet Sites

FactHound offers a safe, fun way to find Internet sites related to this book. All of the sites on FactHound have been researched by our staff.

Here's all you do:

Visit www.facthound.com

Type in this code: 9781491484227

 Super-cool stuff! Check out projects, games and lots more at **www.capstonekids.com**

Index